Day Three: Husband made No-Bake cookies as encouragement. Somehow, I don't think he truly understands how diets work. In fairness, I let out the air of his tires so he could drive to work faster. Seemed like the right thing to do.

Day Four: Traded bikes with the husband as he has the baby trailer attachment on it. Realized quickly not all bike seats are made equally, but pushed on, heroically. Finished the ride with considerable numbness and discomfort to the lower half of my anatomy. Can confidently say I now know what it would be like if that one superhero, it rhymes with Polverine, gave colonoscopies.

Day Five: Staying hydrated. Really hydrated. Didn't leave the bathroom much today. Not only is hunger my constant companion, now the jumbo roll of Charmin is too.

Day Six: Saved enough calories to eat a S'more with the kids around a small campfire we made in the backyard. Almost had

A few days before, there had been a substantial windstorm. Things previously belonging in trees had now to succumbed completely to a Newtonian law all without our permission. Remember this.

Earlier this spring we purchased twelve fluffy little yellow chicks. Six were sexed and six weren't. That means someone can look at their vents and determine if the sweet downy peepers were boys or girls. Boy farmyard fowl are jerks. Not all boys. Nevertheless, we didn't want more babies, just eggs, and the unknown six ended up being four roosters. The biggest takeaway from this, which has zero impact on this story, is that there are professional chicken butt checkers. Do with that information what you will.

So, we were left with seven pullets and Special. Special was smaller than the others, socially awkward, and probably had an anxiety disorder. She was also asthmatic and wheezed like an elder statesman with a penchant for cigars, Scottish whiskey, then not only is the appropriate response involve much profanity, but loads of vulgarity are also encouraged. At this point; however, I in no way condone telling others to shove things in any orifice unless medically necessary and approved by a health care professional.

I've heard the stories of whole offices of men rendered useless until a female staff member finds the file they're looking for. The phenomenon is called the Magic Uterus. The owner of the uterus is knowledgeable of all things misplaced, lost, and in plain sight. How do you not see the orange juice right there in the door?

The Magic Uterus is the only counter-measure currently available for **MRB**. Not only can you grow people with it, but it also helps Phil find the sizable black tape dispenser. (It's next to the stapler where it's always been kept). It's both a burden and an honor to possess such a powerful organ.

aware of my personal distaste of him. Honestly and him a married man! I just thank my stars that James took a fancy to me when he did or I would have been Mrs. Dolly Burr instead of Madison!

August 23, 1814

I sit here waiting for my husband to return and inform me of what is befalling our Washington City. He is, of course, commanding the troops, but he promised me he would return. I hope the British are not marching on our city as rumors tell. What if the British come *here*? Horrors! The ransom for me would be high, surely. Oh, there is someone at the door for me. Maybe it's James. I will soon return.

Later

It was a messenger sent from my husband asking me to take all his Cabinet papers and send them to Virginia. I did as he wished, but do hope the carriage is not overcome on its way to Montpelier. Where is James? Surely, he'll be here soon and

"Mom, would you like a cough drop?"

"Oh, that would be nice, thank you!

Ugh, why is it all wet?"

"I pre-licked 'em so they taste better!"

down. Breakfast is ready." She served me more orange juice, eggs and toast. She was cordial, almost formal. I was enjoying the treatment but I'd also known her long enough to wonder why the pomp and circumstance. I began eating and watching her move. She had always been athletic – short, squat and incredibly strong. Today she seemed lighter, almost angelic in her movements. Her eggs were fantastic. Liza used to cook this dish she called Hindu Eggs, which in addition to eggs consisted of potatoes, onions, cumin, turmeric and a little red pepper. These particular Hindu Eggs also had zucchini, and with coffee the breakfast was fantastic. Liza was watching me also, and for awhile neither one of us spoke. "Great eggs," I said, finally. She sipped her tea and looked out the window. "Our lease is up in two months."

"Yeah," I said, not knowing where this was going.

"Do you like this place?"

I thought about it. The house had 2 bedrooms, and except for the rare occasions that my band practiced here, there was enough room for both of us. She resented the band practice so we rehearsed there as little as possible. The yard was great for Duke, and the location was decent. "Yes, I like the place. Why?"

"I'm not so sure," she said. "We have awhile to think about it, but I'm not sure if I really want to stay here." I looked at her and I had nothing to say. We'd been together six years overall – from 19 to 22 and then again 24 to now. We got engaged at 22 then split and I moved away. She came out to meet me 2 years later and moved in. The engagement was never officially called off, just put aside until we felt like dealing with it. I vaguely remembered the time in-between the two phases of our relationship. After traveling a bit, I settled in Boulder. I dated rarely and read exhaustively. I was relieved when Liza broke away from mom & dad two years ago to live with me in the mountains in Colorado. I missed her.

"I like it here," I said noncommittally, "but I'm not attached. Colorado is good but not great. Where would you want to go?"

"I don't know, but I've been thinking about it." She rubbed her chin and got up to do laundry. I watched her walk out and I thought about our engagement. Did I really want to marry this girl? Was it love or comfort? We were expert procrastinators, but the time for decision eventually comes – no matter how hard you try to stave it off. I finished the Hindu Eggs, washed my dishes, and went upstairs to take a shower.

As I was brushing my teeth I heard the phone ring. I turned on the shower and looked at the white grimy tiles. I thought about how many people had lived and showered here since this house was built, and about the sense of permanence I knew Liza wanted that I could never provide. At least not yet, not now. I toweled off and went into the bedroom to dress for work. Liza was putting her clothes back in the closet.

"That was my Dad. They're coming out here in two weeks. I told them they could stay in the den."

"What about the dog?" Liza's mother was petrified of dogs. And Duke weighed 92 pounds. He was a black lab/Newfoundland mix.

"Well talk about it tonight. When are you getting in?"

"My last appointment is 5:30. So probably 6:30 or 7." Liza kissed me. I held her and tried to think about the future, but nothing would come. Just an opaque green haze and a long, dark hallway.

II

Liza was working so I met the Goldsmiths at the Denver International Airport, which is really more of a space hangar or an alien outpost and is not located anywhere near Denver. It was about a 50-minute drive and I relaxed myself with classical music – Chopin and Mozart, to prepare myself for their arrival. I got to the gate with fifteen minutes to spare, and began re-reading "A Confederacy of Dunces," by John Kennedy Toole. I was laughing out loud when the passengers began deplaning, and I saw the Goldsmiths approaching. Mr. G was carrying one bag, and Mrs. G was made up but looked good, like she had come to terms with something, finally.

Upon seeing me Mr. G extended a warm hand, which I shook; and I pulled him in for a hug. A bit surprised, he responded warmly. Mrs. G turned her cheek to me and kissed the air beside my face. "How was your flight?"

"Decent. We had a non-stop."

"Are you hungry? Did you eat on the flight?"

"We snacked. But I could eat. You know how it is with plane food." said Mr. G. His voice had lost none of its volume or intensity.

"Liza will be off at 8:30. It's 7:15 now. We should get the baggage and be home at about the same time. We've already made up the den for you."

"What about the dog?"

"He'll stay in the yard, but if he barks all night I'll bring him in to stay with me."

We got to the baggage claim without incident, loaded the trunk and drove back to Boulder without a hitch. I explained my work environment, my plans and my goals, which were received quietly and without scrutiny. Either my aura was less confrontational nowadays or the Goldsmiths had begun to accept me as part of Liza's life. When we opened the door Duke came to greet us. He jumped up and I took him by the collar and put him out back. I came back in and Liza was there, she came home right after we did. There they were, the three Goldsmiths, and my vision tunneled a bit. I tried to picture going to the Goldsmiths' house for holidays (children in tow, dog in kennel), and shook it off. I went back to the hallway and helped Mrs. G with her luggage.

So here they were again, two years later. And how much had really changed? Liza and I were still involved yet quietly non-comittal. We had evolved a bit spiritually, and were definitely more accepting of ourselves and each other, but nothing ever happened for either of us. No monumental event like an avalanche or an earthquake, to reassure us that this relationship really was the right thing. And on it went, until the Goldsmiths arrived for their second and final visit.

The first night Mr. & Mrs. G were tired, so I ordered in sandwiches & salad from Buffy's Deli and we ate at home. Duke stayed outside, and all was pleasant. I talked about my M.F.A. program with enthusiasm, and Liza talked about enjoying her time in Colorado, but feeling that in the long run it was probably not her home. She said she missed New York a little but wasn't willing to fight for oxygen and elbow room on the subway at this point in her life. Mr. G told a few wild stories about his school, and Mrs. G talked about antiques and her friends' travel plans. We planned a trip to Nederland to go antiquing. We opened a bottle of chianti I had been saving and the night went off without a hitch.

The second day (which was really the first morning) we woke up early, it was a Saturday. We made coffee and laid out the itinerary – a morning hike, then they would drop me off at home and get a rental car. After that I would go to band practice while the Goldsmiths went antiquing in Nederland. We would meet at Toro Sushi at 7pm.

With our plans set, we went to Fred's for coffee and bagels, and then up Flagstaff mountain. To give the Goldsmiths quality time together and me a chance to walk my dog, I took the loop trail and gave them the car, making arrangements to meet them at the trailhead in an hour. I walked slowly, as if in a dream. The fall foliage was evergreen and yellow, not the rustic reds and oranges of upstate New York where Liza and I had met. It was the rare moment like this, usually in autumn, when I missed the colors of New York. But I had made the break, once before, not only because I was unhappy in New York, but because I never thought Liza could break free from her parents, and I thought a move would entice her. And we keep returning to the same place, Liza and I, a place of noncommittal resignation and steadily improving sex. The psychic communication was never forged, in favor of the committed nurturing of a gymnastic bodily relationship. Sports had been the catalyst with the two of us from the beginning – an athletic attraction and a recognition of the acrobatics of the other.

Duke and I walk on, and finally I let him off the leash and we both wander into our respective lives. Duke can get pretty crazy at times, and I only let him off the leash when I'm pretty certain there's minimal chance of Duke disrupting, damaging or demolishing the surrounding landscape. One time at Mt. Rainier when I was hiking with Chris and two German girls we met at the hostel, Duke nearly got himself killed. He's got this propensity to frantically chase small rodents, and while we were at Sunshine Point I was loosely holding him and talking with the group. Duke spies a chipmunk frittering away a thousand feet down the mountainside and takes off like black lightning, ripping the leash out my hand and charging down the mountain at about 70 MPH. Obviously he got nowhere near the rodent, and because of the high altitude he huffed and puffed his way about halfway back to the overlook where we were all standing, mouths agape, watching this ridiculous spectacle. Duke starts wobbling and collapses with a yelp, passing out and breathing heavily, his big pink tongue with two black spots sticking about three feet out of his mouth.

     Now you're not supposed to leave the clearly marked trails, but my dog was dying, so I trudge down the mountain and after about eight minutes I get to the place where the dog is lying. I am scared that I've lost my dog and worried that the forest service will arrest me for stepping off the marked trail. I get to Duke and scoop his 92-pound body into my arms and struggle up the mountain, stumbling, tripping, almost dropping my dog into the abyss below. Finally I get him to the car and we're out of water!! We had a warm bottle of Sprite handy and I fed him a little Sprite, practically pouring it down his throat. We asked a few hikers in the parking lot for extra water, and for the next two hours I sat with Duke, pouring water down his throat and begging him not to die. He recovered, but never lost his fetish for small rodents.

     And what were the two of us doing anyway (Liza, not Duke)? Was it okay to just be in a relationship that neither of us was certain about? Were the Long Island pressures of marriage, career and family so firmly etched into to our subconscious minds that we had no recourse but to carry out the will of our parents, and their parents before them? So I wandered on like this, feeling less and less in control of my life and my destiny.

At the appointed hour the Goldsmiths met me at the trailhead and we drove back to town. In the car there lurked a hush, and though the morning itself was radiant and quiet, the stillness in the back seat was so palpable that Duke jumped the divider and sat gracelessly in my lap. We got home in silence and the Goldsmiths dropped me off, barely saying a word. I looked at Liza on my way out of the car and cocked an eyebrow. She looked at me blankly so I closed the car door and went inside with Duke. I showered and got ready for my rehearsal. At rehearsal I went through the motions, but my instincts were telling me to go home. We took a break and I talked to Jeff, the drummer, about what I was feeling. We agreed that I should go home, and the band would finish the rehearsal without me. I drove quickly, abstractedly, back down to Boulder. I got home to find a red and white U-Haul on the front lawn and the three Goldsmiths carrying boxes full of Liza's things, stacking them in piles in the bed of the U-Haul. Duke was running around them, barking and yipping. I got out of the car and looked at Liza, who returned my bewildered glance with with such a look of existential apathy that I had no choice but to accept the inevitable. "Why didn't you tell me?" I offered weakly, but I knew that there was nothing I could say, or even should say. Our time was done, and that was the end of the conversation.

I watched Mrs. G carrying the tiny boxes, barely containing her smile and her sense of personal victory. I had an urge to get my plasma gun, but I had left that in a dream some time ago and it was not readily available. From the front lawn I watched the three of them dismantle what I thought was my house, holding Duke still and staring with a glazed eye up to the dauntless Colorado sky. When every box was packed and loaded, Liza came inside to check the house. I watched her as if through a tunnel. She seemed satisfied, not the least bit remorseful or sad. When she knew she had all her belongings

she handed me a check for the last two months' rent (signed by Mrs. Goldsmith), kissed my cheek, and walked out of the house. She climbed into the U-Haul and I watched them drive off without a good-bye.
I put the dog inside and made some coffee. While it was brewing I picked up a copy of The Brothers Karamazov and turned to the dog-eared page where I had left off the last time Liza left me. Winter was on its way.

Obligatory Y2K poem

Millennium turning
        a glitch here
                there   maybe
but the wheels keep turning
        churning out our false
                perceptions of a Master
long dead coupled
        with an inaccurate birthdate and
        old Constantine
        must be laughing from his fiery pit.

Apocryphal smiles and silicone tits
        Hollywood ahead by three lengths
                with the people closing in fast

binary blizzard and we without snowshoes
        grapple with speed unfathomable
                acceleration unnatural
like a curtain pulled up
to
        reveal
                          a
                                vortex
    where
            a   stage
                      should
                          have been

since Roswell (after which the transistor suddenly and
miraculously showed up) the rules
have changed and you
are willingly
kept in the dark.

Sift
if
you
feel the need
through

abduction stories
implant stories
encounter stories
but if you've never been visited (while awake)
how do you know?
what do you trust?

Enter Hollywood (again) with
ID4 and MIB
cute little hooks and slight transmutations
so visually stunning (and incredibly expensive).

And through disappearing Mars probes and
genetically bizarre foodstuffs
the promise is huge - medical miracles
and scientific breakthroughs,
the world of music opening up, artists on display.
The Internet is the
people doing ---
creating, replicating, saving tiny pieces
for an uncertain posterity.
the Net is the beautiful chaos of millions of people
billions of ideas
trillions of bytes
but not all this embryonic human fodder
at the end of an imaginary century
can begin to comprehend countless galaxies
boundless universes

our minds are still
too small too unprepared
too thoroughly entrenched
too murderous too infantile
too unconnected to our hearts
but one by one
we have no choice
but to awaken
to the vastness
we have no choice
but to awaken
to the Love

7 Jan 2000
Richmond ,VA

Taciturn
(2001)

Taciturn

185 Poverty Line
188 On the Being of Us
190 In This Vortex
191 Call Her Sylvia
192 Baby's Theme
194 The Fatal Kiss
196 Widow Sketch
199 Mexico Impressions #1
200 First Communion, Chimay
204 Jesus' Lament

Poverty line

I'm standing on my tippytoes
and still I can't reach it.
    farming out my soul to three
    institutions of elementary and
    pre-elementary education
children sifting like sand through my fingers.

These days it seems three
jobs isn't enough
Yes I can
pay the rent
and the utilities
and the car payment
(but health insurance?)

and I write this from a restaurant
    so in a sense
        I have it
           really
                good

a bed
a roof
3 jobs plus
students in the eves
in a sense I am succeeding
teaching
being present & somewhat stable
I GIVE
I LOVE

at work I am
compassion incarnate because
these little souls need little blessings and so few
are willing to give

And there is a selfish aspect too, of course,
that keeps me working,
   frantically pedantic,
as one group of
   children transitions
      to another

I take solace, still,
   in kind green Sundays
      and dreams
         of another life
         in another country
         but
all truth lies within and this life is all we have

And that poverty line
   that lurks ethereally overhead
   is someone else's calculation
      of my net worth
and just because they do not value the children
that does not mean I do not value the children

So the food comes and I indulge.
I am rich.

Maybe I won't be making that trip to Mexico this year.
But I've stashed
a little here
a little there

Faith is about
   waiting
      &
         seeing.

12 Mar 2000
Scalo's
ABQ, NM

On the Being of Us

sweet elixir
   like lilacs burning --
your tongue,
   like calligraphy,
      like the epicenter
of an unnamed.
   earthquake.

Centuries unwind
   in our dovetailed embrace --
vague recollections of
   utterances reiterated
and lifetimes forgotten.
   Brazen cliché.

I trace your tongue, your
   teeth with my eyes.
you respond slowly,
   enunciating
as if
   you had written it all yourself.

And I, so long alone,
   consumed
      subsumed

totally unconfused
        unconfounded --
startling clarity
   fills my being
as you slide
delicately
up
down
through
my incarnate history.

Blessed mystery
need we ask why
   as sweet red wine
blurs my edges
   warms my heart
      frees my fingers.

And in this stilling
of time
be willing,
bird of paradise,
to open
   to the beckoning of this
      hot
        desert wind.

In this vortex
   where words stand
      like a naked handmaiden
   poetry is a deep harmonic
      beyond voluptuous rhythm
         pedantic rhyme
   Even screaming is no defense
      as anger fails/falls away
         fear sucks in its gut
      to take one last punch
        and knows it is beaten.
This slow, steady pulsation,
  older than time,
    is in fact perhaps
       what we modeled our paltry
          linear time after.
  And how hollow that has become!
       our circadian rhythms shifting
         from a cool agrarian surrender
            to a tepid technological travesty

And when alarm clock plucks you
     mercilessly from sleep
        will you remember
            that place
            of wordless harmony
            unfathomably
                beautiful surrender?

29 June 2000
Burt's Tiki Bar, ABQ, NM

Call her Sylvia

Impenetrable gypsy
   fluid grace
there is nothing to perfect
   but the way I watch you move

And where is there to go, for you,
   in this desert night
   tucked away in a desolate
   corner of a nation
that worships its obsessives,
        its steroid freaks
        its adolescent heroes

From some dark European wood
    you appeared in this wasteland
    summoning with your frantic bow

These three-chord cheese doodles
   in the throes of rock-n-roll ecstasy,
    can they see you in the
       lightning, in the dark of the wood,
      your viola giving its
        song back to the trees?

29 June 2000
Burt's Tiki Bar, ABQ, NM

Baby's Theme
(for Jessica)

D.H. Sherman

The Fatal Kiss

The fatal kiss is the one not given. You've thought about that moment repeatedly - a crossbeam of light across her face, her acquiescent eyes in the stairwell at a friend's house, and you know you want to kiss her. You lean, hesitate, and the moment is gone. Pain like a vacant memory stirs in you and you repress it. You see that corner in her friend's house when your lips and souls were close but you never kissed her and there she is -- a butterfly, a magnet.

You have recreated the moment so often, in masturbation, in fantasy, with infinite undulating permutations. She has been a goddess, a cobra, a crocodile, a litany of deity in a distant linguistic. You do what you can to stay composed.

She is screwing somebody else right now, and you know that your intention is really not to get her into bed. You want something more irrevocable; you want to flashbulb her heart. X-ray her for one beautiful and suspended moment and transmit your inner essence, pour out at the core. You want to show her what she missed when she failed to kiss you in that corner in that house. You turned it into her loss because anything else would have been too difficult. But you know you hesitated, jumped, and she was gone again.

You've made progress artistically, made more friends, had three short relationships with varying levels of commitment and intensity, but it is her kiss you have deified throughout the duration.

You see her before she sees you, and you quicken and race. Your gait speeds up a step and when she looks up you are already looking at her. Your recognition is quick and your enthusiasm high. You go directly to hug her, leaving her no choice but to talk. You look at her and she appears genuinely happy to see you. You talk and laugh for four or five minutes and you are staring at her lower lip, the one that pulled you in and you hesitated, the one that has filled the void in so many fantasies. She tells you she's late for class and begins to walk away. You ask her to go out for coffee. She says she doesn't drink coffee but she has your number. She flutters away, and you are left to remember the fatal kiss.

Widow Sketch

Usually I only see the widow at night, but today she appeared in the conservatory in late afternoon, in broad daylight, checking her e-mail and riffling through her bills. She was wearing short sleeves and jeans, her pale arms fluttering, actually expressing joy. Now and then she glances toward my window, but I don't know if she's aware that I watch her.

I imagine that in some way my discovery of her husband dead of a heroin overdose on the couch brought us closer. She spent that night in my house, crying and holding my hand or hugging me for support. Bachelor that I am, I couldn't help but feel the softness of her breasts, her total surrender to her agony. Since that night, my attraction to her has grown, and I fancy myself her guardian. So, from my window, I watch.

It was only two months before she did something with the life insurance money. She bought a new red jeep. I see it parked in the driveway and I wonder how quickly her pain subsided — when she realized that she was free.

When she waters his flowers, the ones he took such meticulous care of, I am able to see beyond my own desire; I am aware that she is still hurting, may always hurt. But if I see her I will stop in the middle of my daily walk, or whatever I am doing, to talk to her. I fancy myself a little beacon in her life, providing humor, comfort and companionship. Now and then, we talk about him.

"Pete had been faking urine tests routinely, the doctor thought," she said. "Freezing urine and reheating it in a microwave." I was truly surprised. I had never seen a heroin addict in such good spirits, or, for that matter, take such good care of his lawn.

"I didn't see the needle when we checked the house," I said, "but the police found it in the kitchen. I guess I was nervous. First dead body." I looked at her then, at her soft, speckled eyes. She had left him when his heroin use got out of control, and was staying with a sister when he died. She never saw the body - the grotesque posture, ass in the air, face on the couch, arm dangling by the window sill, as if he were crawling to the locked window for air. Those white fingers splitting the Venetian blinds, limp, lifeless, were my only clue that something was amiss.

I used the key Pete left me and went in. The house was meticulous, save for a can of shoe polish on the coffee table and his brown shoes on the floor. It looked like a typical Thursday night, Pete about to shine his shoes for work the next morning. Yet there he was, in his underwear, socks and T-shirt, dead at least six hours, his blood pooling and his face ghastly shades of white, purple and blue.

Polly belongs to Pete; and I know that my fascination for Polly stems from that. You see, Pete belongs to me now, too. Though I don't belong to him, and never have. I found him after he took the final needle. He was long gone before I ever arrived on the scene.

Whenever I see her, I nudge the imagined intimacy I feel for Polly along. I'll greet her with a hug, engage her in animated conversation. Her intensity level varies. We've had some good talks, Polly and I. And that, perhaps more than anything else, is responsible for my feelings toward her, and my need to watch.

By night, she is seated at her computer. By day, while I'm away, she is in the garden, meticulously keeping Pete's lawn alive.

Mexico Impressions #1

There is a spirit no photo can capture
    the pulse of the music
        the romance in the language

Beautiful dark women carry their burdens stoically
    timeless old women, three feet tall
        in worn old flowered skirts with hands
            stronger than a man's
    these are Mexico's warriors.

Time passes in breaths, in eons, in the
    interplay of rain and sun.
When dark brown eyes meet mine
    I am humbled, astounded by
    quiet strength in wounded hearts.

Distant impoverished eyes, trained
    to knife the gringo heart,
    beg for pesos on filthy archaic streets.

Craftsmen here are masters, living
    testaments to time and patience.
    I stare, dumbfounded, as the clay
    shapes itself in their hands.

And words? Words here come slowly from my pen,
    like the child first learning to write.

First Communion, Chimayó

In Love's holy fire
        and an overpacked vehicle
we drove - two New York Pilgrims
        dissolving our exile.
This Northern New Mexico sky
        overwhelming us in silence,
in feelings of bestowal.

When the road forked north of Santa Fe it was
        almost a whim I spoke.
"Have you ever been to Chimayó?"
She said no and we took the high road to Taos.

Since 1814 when construction began
these brown-skinned people of the earth have walked
through crystal blue skies and
(until recently) unpaved desert to
        pay Jesus with
        the calluses of their devotion.
I do not know exactly when the missionaries
came through here and
convinced the people that this white-skinned man,
hairier than any of his (relatively) new ardent followers,

had come and gone
>so they could come and go,
>>and never worry.

Even my lover in tears with her omnipresent camera was
>blind to the depth of these
>followers of the bearded one,
fruits of family trees ancient and abundant.

And I, with a cheap Americanized name
and no great-grandfather,
>stare transfixed at these orange Chimayo hills and
>haven't even the capacity to weep for my lost heritage
>- I am too modern, too numb.

We pull into the Santuario, it is her first time.
>I have been there before - to ply my
>hands with holy dirt and read the names of the
deceased in the bearded one's eternal care.

I have even prayed there, a Jew coming home in a place
>holier than religion.

It is really like that in Chimayó, in this Santuario,
for these walls house the million little steps

of the haunted pilgrims
who have come through time
> to pray from hearts more broken, rich and tortured than I
> in all my wonderbread affliction
> can ever begin to fathom.

She is drawn to the pigeons in the makeshift cupola - she
> senses their stoicism, their homing instinct.
> And as she
> clicks her shutter my eyes wander

to the distant hills and the weather-beaten walls.

We go inside, eventually, past the plaque for the unborn,
> past the holy water
> of which she partakes. I do not.

The rickety old pews house weekend travelers, people
> who come out of curiosity or devotion.
> The little old reverend in his
> white garments with fancy names
> conducting a trilingual mass.

The Latin Spanish English flow together in a babble I
> transform into conversation with my god.

I look up at the *vigas* in the ceiling and marvel at
> these little brown people
> with hearts like lions,
> who understand the bearded one more
> than those lost missionaries who
> gave them the word all those years ago.

I marvel at their crude hand-carved effigies, their
> indomitable will to survive.

In deference to these unknown warriors, these pilgrims
> and these builders,
> this tortuous fate that brought me to this desert,
> I stand in line with my lover to receive
> the wafer, which dissolves like hope into my mouth.

At the appropriate moment I rub Chimayó's holy dirt
> into my hands, my third eye.
> I have received the body of these people.
> For a moment I am a Jew transformed.

Jesus' Lament

In the great hall of unceasing meditation where great souls incubate between lifetimes, Jesus sat, discorporate, and inhaled. With his tendrils of infinite awareness he located those souls on the earth plane calling for his help, and with his incredible compassion assisted them with the healing power of his love.

In his meditation, he talked to God in the unspoken language, and tried to free himself of his burden, which in the past three hundred years or so had grown heavier and heavier on his heart. Though he was too compassionate to truly complain, in the language of his heart he yearned to know when his mission would end. He enjoyed the first seventeen hundred years of being a light which the downtrodden and disillusioned could call upon in distress, but he admitted to himself that it had all become a bit narcissistic.

The time had come in his heart to transcend the role of savior and move on to other things, but with so many people relying on his eternal compassion and infinite love, he felt irresponsible just abandoning ship. So he talked to God in the language God understands and he asked how to be true to himself without being selfish. He asked whether there was a way to bring the people into a greater illumination, thereby rendering the role of Jesus obsolete. The truth of the matter was that two thousand years was a long time to sit at the desk of eternal bureaucracy filing through and stamping soul complaints, and the long years of hard, uninterrupted work had soured Jesus' attitude from one of true compassion into one of honest bewilderment.

It is a testament to the greatness of his soul that he was not bitter. He had gotten over the fact that his own people not only had failed to recognize him, but had actually rewritten a large portion of their history to exclude him. In fact, he realized only a few hundred years after leaving the earth plane that rewriting was a basic human trait; and that anything written and rewritten by human hand, by default, was a step further removed from the original wisdom that He as soul and savior had tried to bring to the people when he incarnated and walked among them.

So in his soul there was room for laughter at human folly, but also a genuine anguish at the repetition of human mistakes and the interminable cycles of human history. "If they would only follow a little simple advice," he would complain to God in the unspoken language, "so much useless destruction could be avoided."

God, for his part, sensed the internal souring in the lament of Jesus, and as a remedy tried to console him with memories of all the people who had truly bettered their lives by using Jesus as their example and their inspiration. But God knew, though Jesus was too humble to ever say it or even let it cross his mind during meditation, that Jesus was burnt out on the endless human drama, and needed new horizons to uplift his spirits. God saw the incredible workload that Jesus took on, and admitted to himself that not even He, God, realized that Jesus would have a two thousand-year job description.

Compared to saints of India, holy men of Tibet, and the scattered shamans in the remote corners of the earth who did their jobs leaving their imprints to raise the vibration of the consciousness of their people, Jesus had a really rough time. Out of all the Masters that God had sent down through the ages, not a single one had done more for his people after leaving the earth plane as had Jesus. God admired the tenacity of his holy child, and in his own way sympathized with his lament. He told Jesus this with a touch of fatherly empathy, for there was really nothing he could do.

Until the people who relied on Jesus for love, compassion and salvation took matters into their own hands, Jesus was obligated by heavenly contract to mediate their claims to God. Jesus, understanding this intuitively and with infinite compassion, exhaled, and prepared himself for the ministration of the next batch of souls calling his name.

ABOUT THE AUTHOR

David Howard Sherman was born in Brooklyn and raised on Long Island. He is currently the director of the Atitlán Music School in Guatemala.

After an extended stay in New Mexico, Mr. Sherman embarked on an international teaching career in 2006, and has lived and taught in five countries on four continents.

As Sherm Davis, he is an author, songwriter, and occasional journalist and photographer.

by Sherm Davis

Learning to Stutter (a novel)

The Hair Collector and Other Stories
(La recolectora de cabellos y otros relatos)

Lost Century Compendium
(PoetryProsePlaysPieces 1992-2001)

ALL WORK © EYEBOX PRODUCTIONS IN PERPETUITY.

www.ingramcontent.com/pod-product-compliance
Lightning Source LLC
Chambersburg PA
CBHW022357040426
42450CB00005B/218

Petting the Cat with Marshmallows

Petting the Cat with Marshmallows
Questionable Parenting Practices for Modern Times

Kindle Direct Publishing

Seattle, Washington

Copyright © 2020 Angela Christie

All rights reserved. No part of this book may be reproduced in any form or by any electronic or mechanical means, including information storage and retrieval systems, without permission in writing from the publisher, except by reviewers, who may quote brief passages in a review.

This is a work of creative nonfiction. The events are portrayed to the best of Angela Christie's memory. While all the stories in this book are true, some names and identifying details have been changed to protect the privacy of the people involved.

Publisher's Cataloging-in-Publication Data

Christie, Angela, 1982-
Petting the cat with marshmallows : questionable parenting practices for modern times / Angela Christie.
Seattle, WA: Kindle Direct Publishing, 2020.
LCCN: 2020916481 | ISBN: 978-0-578-75506-9
LCSH Christie, Angela. | Motherhood--Anecdotes. | Motherhood--Humor. | Parenting. | Parent and child. | Humor. | BISAC HUMOR / Form / Essays
Classification: LCC HQ759 .C527 2020|
DDC 306.874/3--dc23

Cover design and images from Canva by Angela Christie

Printed in the United States of America

Published by Kindle Direct Publishing
410 Terry Ave N, Seattle, WA 98109

www.AngelaChristie.com

This book is for everyone who wanted me to.

You asked for it.

"Our life is frittered away by detail... simplify, simplify."
Henry David Thoreau

Contents

Acknowledgments -xi

Introduction-xii

A Guide to Life with Children -1

Custodians of Memory- 5

21 Day Diet- 9

Great American Census- 13

How to Be the Best Mom Ever- 17

A Penchant for Cigars and Scottish Whiskey- 21

African Kittens- 27

A Day on the Farm- 29

Male Refrigerator Blindness- 33

The New Forty- 35

Dear Yoga Pants- 37

Dating and the Modern Prude- 39

Smell This Spot- 43

Diary of Dolly Madison- 45

Fleeting Beauty- 49

My Big Fat Legal Abortion- 53

B.O.A.T.- 55

Flag Day- 59

Running a 5k: A Horrific Journey with Calorific Results- 61

Communism and the Modern Parent- 65

Go to Your Room- 69

Love in the Time of Corona- 73

Animal House- 77

My Favorite Octogenarian- 81

Salted Caramel; or, The Downfall of Modern Civilization- 83

Censored- 85

Damn Applesauce- 89

The Cereal Bowl- 91

The Bears I Dream of- 93

Cleaner, Clearer Windows- 97

Defense Against the Domestic Arts- 99

The Saints' Patience- 101

The Cats in My Dryer- 103

Paparazzi- 105

Unequally Yoked- 109

Night Maneuvers- 113

About the Author- 117

Acknowledgments

At this point, the author would like to acknowledge all of those who helped make this glorious work a physical manifestation of greatness and not just thoughts flitting around for an occasional social media post.

Firstly, the children were a great asset as they all contributed to the bulk of the material as well as kept the author from writing with constant interruptions and general neediness.

The pets adopted have also proved a great source of general mayhem.

Secondly, this work was edited by freelance volunteers who deserve much recognition. Mary Ellen Holmes and Diana Christie, to whom the author is related, must receive lots of credit. All mistakes herein are the author's own.

Lastly, the English teachers and professors who offered support and encouragement; a few going so far as to suggest a master's degree in creative writing should going back to college ever happen. You make a difference.

Thank you.

Introduction

World domination was never my goal, but it was always my intention.

"But, Angela," you say. "You don't even have domination over basic hygiene let alone the world."

Baby steps. Rome wasn't built in a day and never shaving isn't just for November. I maintain that a luxurious coat of excessive body hair adds insulation and doubles as camouflage during hunting season.

There's really no time for rigorous hair removal and maintenance when your child, who begged for a snack of plain, cold marshmallows of regular size and color, can now be seen sitting on the couch stroking the eldest kitty on the head with a white confectionary blob.

"Are you petting the cat with marshmallows?" You ask, making sure what you're seeing is indeed your current reality.

An enthusiastic little voice replies, "Yeah. She likes it!'

This book was created purely to entertain and delight. Its goal is to make you feel better for having read it and possibly want more, at which time you will beg the author for a sequel, but not for cold plain marshmallows to rub on the cat.

A Guide to Life with Children

1. Do not engage in sexy-times with your other. Children and even babies have built in sensors that alert them the minute your husband tries to put the moves on you. Immediately they will start crying even if they previously appeared comatose in slumber. They'll say they want a new brother or sister, but I don't know how they expect this to happen when they keep interrupting.

2. Don't buy anything white. Forget white blouses and never, ever indulge in white pants. Don't get the white sheet set even if it's for yourself because somehow, they will get stained/ruined. Don't fool yourself into thinking a white shower curtain is safe. It's in the bathroom, right? They should be naked and clean-ish. WRONG! Somehow, someone will spill a spiced chai latte on it.

3. Don't buy new furniture until the last kid moves out. I have cleaned so much pee, puke, and foodstuffs off our furniture that I'm just going to burn our living room set as soon as it's feasibly possible. It's not going to charity. Those poor people have enough problems without my couch added to it. I recommend throwing a decorative quilt over the stains and pray to all that's holy your company has a poor sense of smell.

4. Do not indulge in the vehicle of your dreams. Just spray the backseat down with some of that spray-on truck bed liner stuff and (again you're going to need to invoke a whole lotta Jesus) pray for the best. I think the best solution is a police car with a sound-proof divider, but I'm told those aren't available to the average citizen.

5. Don't ever say what's really on your mind- even if you think the kids aren't listening. They are listening-always. It's like having tiny, unqualified CIA agents around all the time. The only time they aren't on high alert is when you say their name

and are actually addressing them. They will repeat what you said to everyone at every opportunity at top volume.

6. Don't buy your kids expensive, name-brand clothing. If by some great miracle they don't rip holes in it by the end of the month, they will have outgrown it by then. I have choice, unflattering adjectives for parents who do this. If you want to dispose of your money so badly, you are perfectly welcome to throw some cash my way. I will even send a self-addressed stamped envelope.

7. Don't even try to indulge in "me time" during the day. Or any time really. The exact minute you sit down with a cup of something good and begin reading a tiny magazine article after you actually got dressed for the day i.e. put on a bra, the toddler will have pooped on the hall rug and the eldest will have gotten stuck behind the couch. After you clean up poop and are helping the eldest, the toddler will have gotten a hold of the dozen eggs you just bought and will be joyously breaking

them all over the fresh laundry. You need to stay on high alert at all times. Don't relax. Don't let your guard down.

8. Don't expect to indulge in adult movies ever again. No, not THAT kind of adult movies! I mean movies that aren't animated; that actually involve some kind of dialog and/or plot. People who are singing, dancing, and interspersing with didactic questions don't count.

9. Don't ever go without hard-soled footwear in the living room. The Lego your tender digits will encounter make fire walking seem like a spa day indulgence.

10. Don't give up hope. I'm told it goes by fast and it's worth it in the long run. Hopefully, your sanity will return someday.

Custodians of Memory

There are great teachers: really stellar individuals who make a difference and encourage. They're tough enough to make you try harder but kind enough to keep you from being discouraged. There are also teachers like Mr. P. I'll never know what I did to make him hate me so, but he never liked me. He could have been just another teacher I had in high school. Instead, he made himself, so disagreeable that when I hear his name, I think, "ugh, that idiot."

It began in 10th-grade algebra. Mr. P's job was to COACH SPORT and he took this very seriously. He was chummy with all the athletes in his class. He'd joke and tease. His real job was to, of course, teach high school algebra. In a small, rural community though, SPORT is all-encompassing, all-consuming, and all that matters in life. If he'd been this dedicated to education well, this would be a different story.

Each class was always the same. He'd lecture for about ten minutes about the lesson, assign the problems he wanted us to finish in the particular chapter of the book, and we'd get to work. I had finished my homework early. I neatly tucked it my math book and took out a juicy piece of fiction and settled in for what promised to be a solid twenty-minute chunk of reading time.

Now I could have starting passing notes. My best friend was in class with me and we loved to chat. I could have started flirting with whatever Axe-drenched hominid was nearest. I could have caved to my inner rebel and tagged the desk with graffiti, but no. I read. I sat quietly and was well behaved.

"Angela!" An audible gasp was heard from everyone. "See me after class." I was bewildered. What had I done? What was going on? My stomach started to hurt and I felt sick. I now know it was anxiety and the amount I experienced wasn't normal. My heart was bounding in my chest and I had no idea what I was going to say. The adrenaline rushing through my system made me start shaking. The bell rang and as everyone else filed out, my friend shot me a look of sympathy. Some snotty girl had to chime, "Ooooo! Angela's in trouble."

I walked up to Mr.P's desk. "When I assign you homework, you're supposed to work on it. Not read."

"But I did the homework," I explained.

"Bring it here." He demanded. I got the book and showed my work. He looked it all over and huffed. "Well. You're not going to learn anything by reading." Now, dear reader, at this point he was getting pretty worked up having found nothing to punish me for. I pray to God to this day he meant you're not going to learn math by reading, but even that's a sad and weak excuse because reading is super-important for EVERYTHING WE DO.

"If this happens again, you'll go to the principal." I was curtly dismissed and just as bewildered as ever.

He shot out of the classroom and, I would find out later, made a beeline to the Scholastic book fair in the middle school where my mom was volunteering so he could complain to her about my atrocious behavior. She was just as confused over the whole situation as I.

I didn't learn much algebra in that class, at least nothing I retained, but I did learn that there are ignorant, small-minded people whose grasp on power is so important that they'll say and do bizarre things to keep hold of their power. The ridiculousness of the whole situation was not lost on me. The unfairness of it all is what really rankled. I read somewhere that writers are the custodians of memory. So, while I may not learn anything from reading, my side of the story is known now. And Mr. P is still an idiot.

The 21 Day Diet

We will not discuss the reasoning behind this diet at this time. Just know there are justifiable concerns present to modify one's calorie intake.

Day One: Remained under given calorie count. Didn't go for a mile walk as it was raining all day. Currently so hungry I could gnaw off the dog's back leg and if you could see her meaty haunches, you'd agree they put most 4-H steers to shame.

Day Two: Walked one mile in approximately 40 minutes. Was outstripped by butterflies, snails, and dead soggy worms as others in the party had to examine all tracks in the mud created from yesterday's rain and the hike turned into CSI Woodlands as a cracked, empty painter turtle shell was discovered. Many hypotheses discussed. Optimal heart rate never reached.

an eye poked out with a sharp, flaming, gooey stick. Baby did get a gooey stick stuck in her hair. The middle child burnt himself. While I was helping the others, the eldest dug his stick into the center of the hot ash and coals and proceeded to fling it with more force and passion than Vesuvius.

After the thrilling reenactment of the last days of Pompeii, I needed something to calm my nerves. Another S'more seemed to help. Maybe just one more to head off a building anxiety attack. I'm sure the Italians would agree there's nothing like ashes and embers raining down to put a diet into perspective.

Loss: Mostly sanity
Gains: More white hair around my temples
Success!

"Mom! I pooped!"

"In your pants or in the toilet?"

"Neither! Look! It's a pyramid! Mom? Are you laughing or crying?"

"A little of both, I think."

Great American Census

I received a postcard in the mail about the 2020 census and being the ever-conscientious American citizen, I went online to fill it out. They asked about our country of origin. Having never lived in any other country and having been born in Michigan, I put American. It was not allowed. I thought I could just say European. No. Where were my ancestors from? Well on my mom's side it's all Sweden. On my dad's side, it's Germany and England. What should I put for my kids? Their dad's family is from Ireland, France, and Greece. Do they really want six countries listed?

I think what they wanted to know was how brown we are. That's another topic for another day, but what it made me realize is that while I love Sweden just as much as the next guy, tack så mycket, I don't bleed lutefisk or filabunk. (No wonder we've never gotten invited to the cookout.) I grew up eating spaghetti, tacos, goulash, tomato soup with grilled cheese,

French toast, and quesadillas-not all at the same time, mind you. I'm not *that* American. I really have no affiliation to another country and I'll die before I let my gastronomy be defined by an ocean crossed three centuries ago. What should have never emigrated is pault or palt. Some families have blood pault or liver pault. In a perfect world, there would be no pault at all.

What is pault? What is it indeed! It is the stuff of potatoes and nightmares. One carby, gloppy ball of ground potatoes mixed with flour, stuffed with fried salt pork inside and then boiled. Each massive gelatinous sphere is placed on a serving plate until a mountain of tasteless balls is brought to the table and passed to eager relatives who love the stuff. They'll slice it in two to make the consumption more manageable and drown the mess in butter. The rivers of butter flow that night.

Usually, there's nothing else served with pault and those of us with sensory issues and an actual palate suffer in silence, having hopefully prepared ahead of time by eating a quick peanut butter and jelly at home.

When my brother would bring exchange students or friends from other countries over, my family would subject the poor soul to this horror. Considering the one kid ate cheese smoked over sheep doo, I'm sure it was a step up, but for the others, I mourned this sad step back in cultural exchange. This dish should be kept in the closet with the rest of the family skeletons, not paraded around and shared with foreigners.

Leftovers are plated. There are always leftovers, and then they're passive/aggressively forced on all who attended with hopeful phrases like, "Fry it for breakfast in the morning. It'll taste really good then." "Does Duane want some for his lunches?" "Better take some more." No amount of pleading or polite excuses will deter your hosts. You'll take a plate of Grandma's Corelle in the green crazy daisy pattern full of cold potato lumps and keep them in the fridge as they turn grey.

And they will turn. An unnatural, unhealthy grey will have those who are unfamiliar with your fridge questioning whether you dabble in the occult. Fun fact: the oxidation of the ferrichlorogenic acid in the boiled or fried potatoes is what does it.

My hearty northern ancestors roll in their graves at the thought of the flicka who claims Swedish on the census but will not eat or endorse pault.

How to Be the Best Mom Ever

Step One: Have something exit your uterus. Experts will confirm that it doesn't matter how the life form exits, what's important is that it's out. All of mine had to be forcibly evicted, having remained tenants long after their eviction notice. I'd recommend an epidural for childbirth. They won't offer you one for motherhood.

Step Two: Keep the small, loud thing alive until you die. Some argue that after turning eighteen offspring are adults and can look after themselves. This is a lie. Mothers will never cut the metaphorical cord. Today mine just asked if we got our land taxes paid. I will be thirty-eight this fall.

Step Three: Realize that steps one and two are not one-size-fits-all recommendations and in reality, no matter who you mother to, you will never do it right; there is no right way.

There is no way to be the best mom because we're human and we err, daily. Hourly if they're toddlers.

Step Four: Throw tablets at them and put on Disney+ while you sneak to the pantry for the secret chocolate.

Step Five: Reach the second realization that maybe the author doesn't know what she's talking about, but eh... chocolate does sound good.

Step Six: Fighting breaks out in the living room. The dog is involved somehow and now there's crying. Abandon chocolate. Consider an anonymous life in Mexico, but the mom body isn't Cancun ready. Break up the fight and promise to make Heart of Te Fiti cookies with everyone. Sell dog to the circus.

Step Seven: Get interrupted by the eldest wanting to watch a YouTube video about Minecraft with the sound on. Be told

Te Fiti is spelled wrong. Google it. It's two words and there's an e.

Step Eight: You're still with me? You're nailing motherhood. You are a goddess.

"God made me? He made Henry? I think He ordered the parts on-line."

A Penchant for Cigars and Scottish Whisky

It never rains, but it pours. If my life had one major theme, it would be this proverb.

If you're not familiar with it, congratulations! Also, we can't be friends. It basically means when bad things do happen, they happen all at once.

We only had our new-to-us pit bull for three days. We named her Pumpkin. Pumpkin hates men. Not all men. She really doesn't like our neighbor. The fact he's a rabid Trump supporter is completely inconsequential I'm sure. Even dogs have their standards though.

Meanwhile on this day, a mile away, an elderly lady with dementia left her house to stroll in the woods for the next twenty-four hours without letting anyone know her plans.

and a deep disdain of stairs. She was my husband's particular buddy who liked being picked up and pet.

It was a Tuesday. That means the mail will be delivered without question. It also means there was a mad dash to the mailbox by everyone six and under living here. By that time, the unending thrum of a low-flying helicopter could be heard as it ceaselessly circled our house, looking for the missing octogenarian. The dog felt this was an excellent time to accompany the kids and start barking at the neighbor who was outside.

It was discovered at this time part of the flock was across the road in the neighbor's ditch. As chickens have no known political affiliation, they're frequent visitors to the neighbor's yard. My eldest son began herding them. The dog kept barking. The helicopter began experiencing an identity crisis and thought it was back in 'Nam, believing it was a Huey during Operation Junction City, I guess.

At this point in the chaos, my second born, clearly not involved enough, falls into the ditch behind the mailbox upon some rocks. Remember the windstorm? It was the head chairperson for the yellow jacket relocation program. Luckily the nest cushioned Henry's fall. It wasn't until I felt a sharp pinch on my thigh that I realized he was being swarmed by Satan's stripy assholes. With a Mariah Carey-esque pitch, he began screaming at a volume that makes ears bleed as the cloud of insects swirled around him.

Meanwhile, Cujo won't let up. The Huey thinks it's time to begin Operation Frequent Wind and land so it can start evacuations. I try to herd everyone back to the house and gain some order or at least something that resembles order. I forget what that word even means nowadays.

After taking pictures of all his bee stings and sending them to Grandma, Henry noticed a chicken on the porch on her back with her feet curled in the air. Special had yielded to the biggest panic attack known to chicken kind and frankly I don't blame her. I'm only jealous she beat me to it.

"Oh, Mom. I just broke the world record for using the most imagination!"

African Kittens

The cute, Christian wife blogs don't mention it. And I'm pretty sure the Mars and Venus people didn't dedicate a chapter to it.

I'm not worried about infidelity or even a puppy-skin coat fetish. If my marriage disintegrates, it'll be because someone left the milk jug with three drops of milk in it and returned it to the fridge. Like that is a totally normal thing to do.

The bread bag twist and tuck is questionable at best, but leaving a single swallow of milk for the next person, who has a handful of cookies and a hankering for a cool, frosty glass of bovine secretion, must go against the Geneva Conventions. It's a human rights violation at best.

I can handle the wadded sock balls that lay on the floor *next* to the laundry basket. I can tolerate a urine encrusted toilet seat, but don't do me dirty and trick me into thinking there's milk aplenty when clearly you and the Devil have been making cream of mushroom lies.

If there'd been refrigeration at the time, there would have been 11 commandments.
"Thou shalt not covet thy neighbor's ass."
"Thou shalt not be an ass and put the empty milk carton back, only to disappoint your wife and have her question her judgment in men hourly."

It's wordy and needs its own tablet, but God would have, without a doubt, added that.

There are starving kittens in Africa. Just finish the milk.

A Day on the Farm

My maternal grandfather is extremely safety conscientious. He helped to instill in me a deep fear of power tools, PTO shafts, and cows.

Grandpa is a farmer and my brother and I naturally spent hours on his farm while growing up. One afternoon, at my grandpa's request, Mom drove us to a local dairy farm the next town over.

I'm not sure if it was a 4-H sponsored event or if Farm Bureau had arranged it, but I spent a terror-filled afternoon learning all about different ways to die or become mutilated on a farm. It could be compared to *Final Detestation* for country kids.

Our instructor introduced himself and the very first thing he showed us was his missing hand. His freaking HAND was missing and in its place was a gleaming silver hook! We'd all seen Peter Pan. We were quite aware of the background involved when one deals with a hook-handed individual.

Next, we were shown, with straw-filled dummies dressed in flannel, why you don't go near a PTO shaft. PTO stands for Power Take-Off. It's how the tractor powers the equipment it hauls. It spins like crazy and doesn't have a guard on it. I just had to look it up on wikipedia.org/wiki/Power_take-off. You're welcome. Ugh...don't read the part about safety on there either. Anyway....

There are also chopper boxes (or forage harvesters) that have "a flywheel with a number of knives fixed to it that chops and blows the silage out a chute of the harvester into a wagon."

Did farmer's feel their image was suffering? Was there a secret meeting? A sun-damaged man swathed in Carhartt stands. "Thank you all for coming. I know it's summer and everyone is really busy. Have you seen the corn out at Eisenga's? But our image is suffering. Everyone just assumes farmers wear overalls and plant tomatoes. We need to really change how everyone sees us. Chicks dig macho guys. I know! A FLYWHEEL WITH KNIVES will solve all our problems!"

The dangers of silage bins suffocating people were expounded upon as well as why you DO NOT make an animal that will one day weigh more than an unholy TON your pet. Not only could it trample you or crush you up against a fence, but there's also the fact it has horns and could gore you.

So, if you ever find yourself saying, "You know, I feel inclined to the agrarian life in a lovely bucolic setting," just remember the hook-handed man and all the ways your cows are going to try and kill you.

"Mom! I can't find Incredibles!"

picks up DVD by son's feet

"Oh, I didn't see it. It was there the whole time?"

"That's okay, you're a guy."

"Yeah, I didn't look down."

Male Refrigerator Blindness

Most of us have experienced it. The pain. The sorrow. The extreme frustration. Sadly, there's no known cure. Sufferers are oblivious to their malady and inflict it on newer generations.

I'm talking about Male Refrigerator Blindness. MRB is found commonly in the male of the human species. It also doesn't need to involve a fridge, but it occurs frequently in the kitchen. Grocery store shelves, a wife's purse, a sizable cat barf pile just millimeters from his foot are also common situations.

Considering that all inanimate objects will never spontaneously jump into the hands of the person looking for them, it's an incurable affliction that will continue in its severity for the life of the infected.

If you too have suffered for years with, "Honey, where are my keys? Have you seen my phone? Where are my sunglasses?"

The New Forty

I was very excited to turn thirty.

I would be taken seriously. I would stop shopping in the junior's section at stores, and I would not be carded when buying alcohol.

I always hear 30 is the new 20 and since that C in algebra totally shattered all confidence I had in my mathematical abilities, I've no doubt it's true. It's like I get 10 extra years so I'm not going to question the validity, mathematics, or relativity of that kind of statement.

30 is great. I love 30, but no one warned me about the chin hairs! Where did these beasts come from? It's not that sweet, delicate peach fuzz either. These guys are thick boar-bristle guerrilla chin hairs that show up during group photos and job interviews.

If wolves really did go door-to-door blowing down houses, I could say with all honesty (and dejectedness because I'm probably stuck in the house of sticks), "No, not by the hair on my chinny chin chin!"

My husband thinks I exaggerate and he can't see them, but I keep my *La Grange* singing skills mad-sharp just in case Billy or Dusty are suddenly struck down and need backup.

I'm on the shady side of thirty now. Forty is just around the corner and no one has clued me in on what horrors are expected during that decade. If it's as catastrophic as the hairs, I'd appreciate a warning.

Dear Yoga Pants

Dear Yoga Pants,

I thought of you today. As I embarked on my third hour of preparing this Sunday's bulletin for the church, some errant bits of jean began to dig into places pants have no right to be. But you, you bring hope to the muffin-topped, the thunder-thighed, and bubble-butted.

I can't wait to see you at the end of my day. And although you've never actually encountered any activity resembling yoga, you don't bemoan that fact. The forgiving stretch and sublime comfort you offer keeps me coming back for more.

I promise the only time we need to be seen together in public is during trips to the one store with questionable business practices and low, low prices where one must blend in.

My love for you is unwavering.

Until Tomorrow,

Angela

"Mom, I need those rocks. I'm gonna throw them at those bees."

Dating and the Modern Prude

I do not have good luck with guys, and I have never had any stellar dates. I've had quite a few outings with boys, but they were all so spectacularly awful that a life alone with 40 cats seemed a viable option worth trying. Surely a virginal spinsterhood was better than subjecting myself to the opposite gender's idea of a good time.

Corey ruined my homecoming pictures. He was a guy from a different school so naturally, he had an air of mystique and also mesquite if his cologne was taken into consideration.

He wasn't much for conversation or even facial expressions so after a lengthy evening of one-sided conversation, it was time for photographs. He reluctantly put his arm around me, as suggested by the photographer, and I informed him with glib sassiness that I didn't bite-hard. (*Austin Powers* was très chic at the time so I have no excuse). He kind of smiled, chuckled a little, and all was well until I got back our 8x10's.

I blamed the pleated khakis he wore. My girlfriends-all of them-argued no. Caught in time forever was Corey's obvious bulgy delight in my quippy unoriginal one-liner. Needless to say, no one received copies of those pictures and if anyone asks the whole event never happened and those photos don't exist.

Mark was next. Mark said a total of three words the whole two weeks we were acquainted. He was really proud of this fact. He also took me to see *Dude, Where's My Car?* on the big screen. I'm going to take a page from Mark's book and just let you know the less said about him, the better.

Another train wreck was Todd. Todd asked if he could kiss me after a case of beer and only knowing me two hours. I reminded him, quite kindly, that we were strangers until two hours ago. Let's face it. Unless you're a dentist, I'm not going to trust you near my mouth after knowing you only two hours. "Is that a no?" It's a no, Todd. Go sleep it off. Bonus points though for asking for consent.

Bill was another unfortunate encounter. We spent the entire evening in his room at his parent's house playing the video game *Silent Hill* and then watching the movie *Jeepers Creepers*. I drove home all alone in the darkest of nights over lonely dirt roads faster than most Daytona qualifiers. I may have ignored most of the traffic signs as I was sure something was coming to harvest my bits because it's a known fact my eyes are way prettier than that kid's in the movie were. Who wouldn't want some of my organs?

I'm glad I don't have to date anymore. It would be even more disastrous if I had to try again as an adult.

"Look, Neil, a police car."

"Catch up to him, Mom, and smoke the doors off of him!"

Smell This Spot

My brother, Zach, has three degrees and is fluent in German. He speaks at least four other languages too. He's lived in Germany and Australia, visited Sweden, Iceland, and camped a whole summer in Alaska. Despite all of this, he maintains the afternoon we played *Sorry* trumps it all.

We were eleven and nine at the time. It was summer vacation and we were bored. We usually spent the whole day outside building forts, but for some reason at this point in the day, we were looking through Dad's glove compartment in his truck. It was there we found a little bottle of cherry-scented air freshener (the manufacturer being very liberal in the definition of cherry) and began spraying every porous surface we could find.

We eventually migrated back inside and began a lethargic game of *Sorry* on the floor of his bedroom. While deeply engrossed in my turn, I was startled by Zach telling me, "Angela, smell this spot." His grubby little finger was pointing to an area on the blue polyester carpet and I, innocently trusting in all things and believing he'd used that cherry spray while I was moving my game piece, leaned over to where he pointed and took a deep breath.

An ungodly stench burned my sinuses and my eyes watered instantly. An odor akin to cabbage cooked in sulfur assailed my senses. I gagged at what was clearly NOT fruity. Satanic giggles rained down upon me and my shame was all-encompassing. My brother had tooted, and taking advantage of my gross naivete, had gotten me to inhale it.

My onetime lapse in judgment has been impossible to live down and if ever my brother brings about world peace and solves world hunger, while he's accepting his Nobel Prize, know that it still does not eclipse that afternoon around the game board when he reached the pinnacle of siblinghood and got his sister to smell this spot.

The Diary of Dolly Madison

I had to do a non-fiction piece in college for an education language arts class and composed this based on a history paper I did for another class. I just really love Dolly Madison.

August 13, 1814

Despite this wretched war, I hosted a fantastic gala last night. Mr. Thomas Jefferson said I had really outdone myself. 'Tis true. Not everyone has the luxury of being able to serve ice cream at almost every social gathering. The ice cream was a delight as the weather was dejectedly hot this previous evening.

James said he was so very proud of me for putting all his guests at ease. It does prove difficult at times- to get all the political parties to stop quarreling for one night of gaiety.

I forgot to mention that the dreadful Aaron Burr was here last night as well, and after all he's done too! I'm sure everyone is what, on God's green Earth, is that confounded racket? I best betake myself outside and see.

1:30pm

Cannons! Good Lord, deliver us! I cannot wait for James any longer. The British are marching on Washington City up the Patuxent River! I better rally all the servants and begin loading up the good silver and china. I will *not* let my good silver fall into the hands of the British!

Later

I have stuffed the carriage to the gills with books, china, silver, eight of the presidential portraits, the Declaration of Independence, and the rest of my husband's documents. My only regret is that we can't take more. My sister, niece, and I are leaving the White House to find a family that will take us in.

It seems no one is willing to give refuge to the President's wife while the British occupy and make war on our fair city.

Humph! We'll see who gets an invitation for ice cream now that their true colors have been revealed. Oh, salvation! My good friend, Matilda Love, has offered to help us flee. Mayhap we will traverse to Virginia.

August 28, 1814 (en route to Montpelier)

I have just learned that the British have burned the White House-MY White House. Of course, 'tis the house of the people, but surely one can understand my frustration. I do hope James and his men give those red-coated scoundrels a thorough beating.

Fleeting Beauty

I thought for the longest time I had beautifully frosted glass light fixtures. The smoky opaqueness would emit a welcoming glow every evening as the living room grew dark and we'd ready for bed. It wasn't until a stuffed animal was torpedoed across the room, hitting the light, and showering us in a thick choking blanket of dust that I realized that the fixtures were not actually frosted. It turns out I'm just a terrible housewife.

The light fixture incident was recalled to me as today I attempted to clean our first-floor bathroom. I do enjoy a clean house. I don't actually mind the physical aspect of cleaning despite my rotund appearance. What really butters my biscuits is that there are four other intellectual, able-bodied people living here as well who are perfectly capable of cleaning too. I can't believe they all suffer from Male Refrigerator Blindness, but they don't seem to notice the colony of spiders living above the sink or the warren of dust bunnies making their home under the toilet tank. If they do notice it doesn't seem to bother them in the slightest.

It was with much grumbling that I started on the bathroom floors. I gathered the bath mat and the area rug in front of the washer and dryer. Sand rained down from the rug in piles rivaling those found in the Egyptian desert. Had it been a year since I did floors in the bathroom? Possibly. Usually, because of the claw foot tub, we prepare for tsunamis, not Middle Eastern-like drought. I should probably feel embarrassed at how much sand fell from the rug, but my chagrin turned quickly to pride as it dawned on me that clearly the Ark of the Covenant was probably in my bathroom the whole time and Indiana Jones was obviously wrong. My unkempt bathroom has the means and wherewithal to house ancient biblical treasures of power.

I don't think my husband realizes how lucky he is to have a partner with a witty personality and a vast abundance of intelligence since these will last me to the end of my days as fleeting beauty was so fleet as to never even arrived. Surely more wit than skills in the domestic arts are what men knock down doors for these days.

"Mom, do you like zombies?"

"No! They want our brains!"

"What about good, little zombies?"

My Big Fat Legal Abortion

When a friend or acquaintance tells me how awful abortion is and how it's murder, what I hear is, "I hate Angela and wish she was dead." Whoa. What? That's pretty extreme, right? It's the truth. My truth. I had an abortion. I *needed* an abortion.

As much as I wish that sweet clump of cells would have been a baby, something wasn't right. It was growing in my tubes and not my uterine lining. I've had two concussions, and cuts that have warranted stitches, but the pain I was in with my ectopic pregnancy was incomparable.

I didn't go to a clinic. An ob/gyn from a prominent medical facility ordered two shots of methotrexate to each butt cheek. Methotrexate stops cell growth. After a week of daily blood draws, bruised arms, and plenty of anxiety, my pregnancy hormone levels were all over the place. They're supposed to rise exponentially. The "baby" wasn't developing correctly.

Was I devastated? You bet. None of my kids were conceived easily and each one was very much wanted. Am I a murderer? Should I have died instead? I could have because I would have ruptured and had sepsis. Was the whole thing awful? Yes, and I know that women who seek abortions aren't doing it for fun. It was terrible.

It breaks my heart to hear people speak from a place of ignorance and without compassion. I'm important enough and good enough to deserve quality medical care and I think other women are too.

B.O.A.T.

"You're the most responsible of all your siblings." They told my husband. Oh, that's nice we said to ourselves unthinkingly. We never expected what came next. One afternoon Bob and Linda came barreling up our driveway and began unhitching what was on the back of their truck. Before we could all pour out of the house, they were giving us the lowdown on what was going on.

They were giving us their old boat. Never mind the fact we had no way to haul a boat anywhere. Our only vehicle at the time was a Dodge Caravan and she could barely carry all our sass let alone the amphibious beast sitting in our driveway.

"It's too small for us." The older retired couple with grown children explained. Our family of five did some quick mental math and as we were scratching our heads at this logic, Bob and Linda drove off to leave us with our new "gift."

Now I've never thought to purchase gloves for someone without hands or shoes for a double amputee, but our being an hour's drive from a substantial body of water and at least twenty miles from enough horsepower to haul a boat didn't stop Bob and Linda. Not for a second.

Linda was under the impression we were going to buy a new truck. Obviously, my secondhand clothing and barefoot children gave her the impression we were rolling in cash when quite honestly the last time I had any greenbacks in my hand was the previous week when the kids had brought frogs from our swamp into the bathtub.

A few acquaintances heard about our predicament. One kind neighbor, bless his soul, told us boat is actually an acronym for Break Out Another Thousand. Well, you can bet your sweet fanny we sold that thing within a week and used the money to buy something we could always use: groceries.

Now and then on hot summer days, of which there are a total of three in Michigan, I think about what might have been, but then I pop open the deep freeze to put away Popsicles and thank my lucky stars Bob and Linda aren't giving us any more gifts.

Flag Day

Someone posted a novella on Facebook the other day about there not being enough American flags flying on Memorial Day. This same person has at least six flags in her yard night and day, rain or shine no matter the holiday so I don't think she could be considered an authority on what's enough.

Many people lamented on her post the fact the Pledge of Allegiance isn't recited in schools anymore. "Back in my day!" They all shout, as if that phrase has ever solved anything. When I start all my conversation with an outraged, Back in my day! everyone has my permission to just send me to the senior assisted care facility and never visit. I know I deserve it.

The author made it seem like the lack of flags meant there was a lack of national pride as if somehow printed fabric, made in China, and displayed in abundance made someone a good American. Now to me, good and American are very subjective adjectives and it would seem, that if they needed to be defined, the definitions would be rooted in deep beliefs and strong moral thinking instead of tangible, inanimate objects.

Why fly the flag? She asks and goes on to explain that it's to remember the bloodshed and lives lost. Having been an Army wife and since I personally know a veteran, I asked my husband, without context, that if he died saving someone's life, how would he want to be remembered.

His answer didn't involve a memorial. It didn't involve eighty flags flown on every national holiday with parades.
"I'd want them to live a good life. I'd like for my sacrifice to have been worth it."

So, to honor veterans, maybe we need to consider that while, yes, Old Glory is indeed magnificent, are we living a good life? It's a lot harder to do than run up another flag, but it seems more sincere.

Running a 5k: A Horrific Journey with Calorific Results

1. Abandon this idea that running = athletic goddess. All the bouncing and wiggling from my front and rear cannot call to mind Diana or Nike. Let's not get carried away. Now a walk. That's manageable for most people.

2. Find a virtual 5k to register for. The company will send you a medal and then you pick your time and place to participate. No need to wake up before all barnyard fowl and congregate with extremely fit individuals who haven't touched a carbohydrate since 2003.

3. Have husband drop you off 3.1 miles away from the house. None of this backtracking stuff. Getting back home to relax and go braless is always a worthy goal.

4. Turn on Spotify workout playlist. Turn on run mapping app. Stuff the earbuds in. Stuff them in again because they keep falling out. Take off at an unbearably uncomfortable sprint because new moms with jogging strollers are judging. Immediately stop jog once out of sight. Try not to wheeze so audibly.

5. Start questioning all life choices. Heart rate is extremely high. Burning fat, no doubt.

6. Shoes start to feel really uncomfortable. Considerably so. Push through the pain remembering Dad's fatherly words of warmth and caring, "Oh walk it off. It's not that bad." Must write next book on childrearing philosophies from the 80s. Push in earbuds

7. Come to the conclusion that Satan himself designed and manufactured the shoes you're wearing for his own cloven trotters as this pain is unreal.

8. Dodge chipmunks as they dart out at you. Start pacing the "run" in chipmunk per minute instead of miles per hour. Dart around green caterpillars hanging from trees on their silk. Inform them they need to stop being gross.

9. Hit mile one. Celebrate with an arm pumping victory yell. Startle cyclists nearby. Push earbuds back in. Who thought this was a good design? Realize Satan has not only taken over footwear but has people in the music industry as well. Fathers of the 60s were right all along.

10. Repeat steps five through nine another mile. Pause running app to fix socks. Kindly turn backside to the woods as not to further startle cyclists. Startle herd of deer instead. Feel guilty at the look of panic in their eyes. Seeing their friends murdered during hunting season isn't as horrific as a Lycra encased rump jiggling in the air.

11. Take five more steps. Realize death is more acceptable than continuing in these shoes. Stare down one really aggressive chipmunk who seems determined to shiv you for your wallet. Take shoes off. Walk two feet. Take off socks. Carry worthless "footwear" remainder of the walk. Push earbuds back in.

12. Complete remaining 1.1 miles barefoot. Arrive home to children and pets spilling from the house, desolate in your absence. Share workout and map with friends. Take selfies with the medal. Order another. Feel accomplished. Push earbuds back in.

Communism and the Modern Parent

My husband purchased a miniature wooden cutting board today. It was to be used in place of our two huge boards that are unwieldy and cumbersome to wash. Was. Tiny Girl, aged 3, saw it emerge from the grocery bag, squealed, "For me!" and took off with it. With a pained look, the guy who puts daddy in daddy's girl said, "I forgot we can't have nice things."

I gently reminded him that we can't have:

1. Nice things
2. New things
3. Things for our own personal use.

We have kids. This is a communist household.

Obviously, we don't share knives or weed killer. And the razors and Tylenol are stored up high, but secret chocolate is a thing now. Why isn't there a chapter in parenting books about hiding the secret chocolate?

My Ipsy glam bags, my one big monthly splurge, are ransacked and pillaged faster than a Norman village near Scandinavia before they're barely out of the mailbox. "Hey, Mom, are you going to use this? It'll be a good case for my phone!" The oldest doesn't wait for an answer as one of our old cellphones, free of its SIM card, now used solely for Minecraft is slipped into a green pleather pouch with studs.

Lone bubble baths are now things of myth and legend. Mom running water in the tub is the heralding call that it's time for a nightly bathroom parade as I help someone with a Wi-Fi password, watch another YouTube video about Minecraft, and keep Tiny Girl from jumping in with me. Heaven forbid if I ask someone to bring me a towel though because suddenly no one is available and all are profoundly deaf.

Now I can hear the authoritarians, whose grown children never call or visit, grumbling, "Back in my day!" We know what I think of that. Also, we don't believe in hitting kids or animals so you'll have to stick that in your pipe and smoke it. All the shoulds, woulds, coulds aren't helpful unless you're willing to come and Mary Poppins for us. Yes, Mary Poppins is a verb now.

There needed to be a chapter in *What to Expect* called I, Me, Mine, and how pure, unadulterated selfishness is going to be a thing of the past. It should probably mention too that only high-ranking government officials are allowed that kind of indulgence.

What's mine is ours and I guess I didn't really need that expensive Santa figurine I got from my aunt as a wedding present anyway. Being able to enjoy the crisp, fresh smell of new couch for more than a month is overrated. Yes, go get a piece of gum from my purse, but throw it away IN the wrapper, alright? It isn't out of the carpet from last time and make sure you share with everyone!

"There are two naughty s-words: stupid and shut-up.

Are there any more, Mom?"

Go to Your Room

My dad and I could not be any less alike. I don't hold that against him. I tried. I think he tried. He was always working so I just don't know. I can't ask either since, well, he's always working. We operate on totally different wavelengths. It was always really easy to make him mad. I know my fuse is pretty short, but Dad's fuse was never installed.

One Halloween night, while we were still little enough to be driven around, Zach and I began to chant about candy bars with an accent. Just to be clear, we had the accent, not the candy bars. We chanted over and over. "Baby Roof! Baby Roof!" Dad about lost his ever-loving mind. Once you know how to push someone's buttons, it's fun to see them light up every time.

Later as a teen, I had checked *Dave Barry's Book of Bad Songs* out of the library and settled in on the living room couch

Sometimes he tried to get us to go haul wood with him. Cutting a load of wood is Dad's all-encompassing, most-beloved passion in life. Any free moment he has is spent cutting wood, splitting wood, hauling wood, delivering wood, getting permits from the Forest Service to cut wood for free on State land, taking the Husqvarna to Ebel's, and it bears repeating, cutting wood. My brother and I were in charge of stacking wood in the truck. Hefty maple logs would fly inches by our heads as Dad tossed them up to us. Expressing concern for our own safety was scoffed at and dismissed with a curt, "I ain't going to hit ya."

Being enrolled in Randy Holmes's School of Tough Love once led me to one of the most triumphant moments in my life, in gym class. It was a co-ed class for upperclassmen. I was in there as a prerequisite and because of scheduling issues. We were playing volleyball and a senior boy spiked the ball so hard, it whistled across the net. Now I had been drilled that the most important rule in sports is to be aggressive so I stopped it with my face. Not on purpose, mind you. Everyone stopped what they were doing. I was met with looks of concern. Did I cry? Did I bleed? NO! I acted like I took sporting equipment to the face on the daily and I kept playing. If Tom Hanks has taught us anything about sports it is that, "There's no crying in baseball." Or laughter from the couch. Actually, any emotion that isn't sawdust just needs to be stuffed back in.

Love in the Time of Corona

I never thought that staying home and having minimal human contact would ever be required of me. Oh sure, I dreamed of it when every open house, baby shower, or wedding invitation popped out of the mailbox, but my greatest desires have actually come true.

Unquestionably, stay-at-home orders felt stifling at first. Just like when I was asked to empty the dishwasher when growing up, my first instinct isn't to politely comply but to balk at the request and refuse to do it until *I* want to.

But my government had called me to action or more appropriately inaction. My duty was never clearer. After changing Internet providers and re-subscribing to Netflix, I readied myself for the rigors of isolation and solitude.

No one told the kids I was on a one-woman mission to keep diseases from taking over, however, so brooding in solitude was going to be best left to Batman. No wonder Thoreau was able to churn out volumes from the wilderness. He wasn't helping people with socks and Wi-Fi passwords. He never had to lather a toddler in sunscreen. Simplify my sweet Aunt Fanny.

The precautions taken to avoid coronavirus haven't changed my life much at all. It's given me a beautiful excuse to indulge in all my favorite anti-social behavior: no touching or hugging and keeping six feet away. It's not because I don't like people either. That's not it at all. It's because I don't understand social cues.

The whole time you're telling me about your trip to Cabo, I'm thinking of all the appropriate responses you expect me to supply. Where should I look? Eyes. That's always the right answer. I need to blink. Gah. I want to blink again. Now I can't stop thinking about blinking. Nod. They like that.

Smile. That's important. I have studied people my whole life. I'm really not shy, I just have no idea what to say or do half the time when I see a casual acquaintance.

I envy people who don't overthink every social interaction and don't freeze with horror when a relative approaches them in the grocery store. A lifetime of crippling social anxiety has finally proven useful. It's my time to shine, normies. Let me have this.

"Mom, moths are just flying triangles."

Animal House

I don't go looking for trouble. All I ask out of life is for lots of quiet, plenty of books, and a bit of nature. Sadly, the universe seems to have run low on quiet for some time. It does deliver when it comes to nature.

Our last house was at one point listed in some animalian AAA guide book as a bat hotel and all weary travelers stopped by to rest during migrations. If I had known, I would have asked to be unlisted as running a bed and breakfast for creatures of the night wasn't something I had the skillset for. However, I maintain to my dying day that nothing will get one to one's optimal heart rate faster and more efficiently than when one is awakened in the dead of night from a comatose slumber by the flutter of wings across one's face.

The local health department suggests you capture the creature, and have animal control come out. If I did that every time something wild came through the door, animal control would never leave. I'd have them on speed dial and we'd all be on a first-name basis. They'd be invited to Christmas dinner and all family reunions, our bond and relationship would be that close.

One evening I awoke to the distressed peeps of a bat that had fallen into a bathtub of water that had been neglected to be drained after tsunami practice. I've been told normal parents call it bath time. Anyway, I used a ceramic coffee cup from nearby and scooped the poor guy out. He was placed on a chair on the front porch to recuperate. Friends suggested I toss the cup because rabies, but upon extensive research, it's only if a bat bites should one worry so #notallbats.

One memorable afternoon the cat casually brought in a very healthy, much alive bunny. We spent a day filled with Vaudevillian antics as we tried to catch a wild rabbit from under the couch. What eventually helped was the construction of a chute of children's toys to the front door and we herded him out like a longhorn steer.

Another time the cat released a live chipmunk inside. I stress the vitality and alertness of each creature as sometimes she brought in things that looked like harbingers of plague. The chipmunk bolted through the living room, into the boys' room, down their register; the grate missing as it was being used as a Star Destroyer, into the ductwork never to be seen again. To this day I often wonder what happened to the chipmunk and since we never smelled anything suspicious, I wonder too how inefficient our HVAC was.

I'm going to start charging these freeloaders rent just as soon as I get the snails out of my bathroom sink and the earthworms stop using my Tupperware® Thatsa® Mega Bowl. Did I mention the monarch caterpillars?

"Neil, why isn't my tape measure working? Did you stuff something in there?"

"Yeah, pussy willows."

"Where did you get pussy willows this time of year?"

"They're in my dresser drawer."

My Favorite Octogenarian

My very favorite person of a certain age is surprisingly not a grandparent of mine. We aren't related at all, but if anything, I feel more love and affection for her than all my grandmas.

It may be because I have no grandmas left and she has fallen into this role at a time when I needed someone the most. I call her my *in loco grandparentis.*

She is spry, sharp, and witty. She tells the best stories and has an answer for everything. One day I was lamenting to her that my family wasn't having a traditional Christian funeral or burial for my recently deceased maternal grandmother. We talked about how funerals are more for the living; those grieving, than the dead.

"Well I'm not getting cremated," She tells me. "I don't care if my girls have to go into debt to bury me. If I wanted to burn, I'd go to hell." It was then I knew she was a kindred spirit.

for a good read. It more than delivered. I would snortle- a combination snort and chortle every two pages, but one part that sent me over the top was the part about *Help Me Rhonda*, and ever since she put me down there have been owls puking in my bed. Immediately I envisioned a four-post bed; owls on each post puking in synchronized glory. Owl pellets raining down on a homespun quilt. I'm giggling now as I write this. What is wrong with me?

My father was trying to read the local newspaper at the kitchen table and yelled at me.

"If you're going to laugh, go to your room!"

What is with people not letting me read? I was pretty miffed because puking owls is freaking hilarious and just because some people have an underdeveloped sense of humor shouldn't mean I had to pack up and read in my room. Eventually, someone gifted me the book and now I can quote it verbatim when the songs mentioned come on in the grocery store. It's a useful but unmarketable talent.

Another time Henry was explaining a cat simulator app to her. "On level ten you get married and on level twenty you have a baby." He told her excitedly.

"I've gotten to level twenty a few times." She replied matter-of-factly.

How does this untapped fountain of sass not have her own daytime talk show? If you don't already have an octogenarian, I recommend you get one and soon. This generation likes to joke about not buying green bananas. Some argue septuagenarians are just as good and more plentiful but trust me it's the well-aged 80-year-olds that offer the wisest mirthful epithets.

Salted Caramel; or, The Downfall of Modern Civilization

I had an unfortunate opportunity to taste something claiming to be salted caramel flavored recently. Immediately it called to mind the salty bile taste I get in my throat just before I barf. It seems too I'm alone in my opinion of salted caramel. "It's so good!" They clamor. I don't know who they are but if vomitus sweets are what everyone craves, more power to them. All I ask is to give the rest of us some other flavor options as well.

I remember as an older teen, during the *Harry Potter* book craze, Jelly Belly (purveyors of very fine jelly beans) offered their take on Bertie Bott's Every Flavor Bean. At one point I chomped into skunk, dirt, and vomit flavored jelly beans. Salted caramel flavored things and vomit jelly beans could be interchangeable in my book.

Most salted caramel stays where it belongs in the dessert aisle, but were you aware they offer salted caramel potato chips? When you're bulking up at the gym, your whey protein can now be sweet, salty, and barf-tastic. There's salted caramel whiskey and when you're regretting the previous night's indulgence, you'll realize that it tasted the same going down as it did coming up and that I was right all along.

This unhealthy obsession for a salty-sweet combination seems to have consumed the culinary world and the hunt for the perfect new flavor will bring about nothing, but chaos and ruin. Next everything will have to be blueberry and cucumber flavored. Apple and pickle flavored whiskey will be on the shelves presently. Just know when the world becomes a dessert wasteland and civilization has collapsed as a result of wars and dwindling resources, it will be because of salted caramel.

Censored

When my grandma passed, my grandpa asked me to write her obituary. I thought Zach was going to be the chosen one so I was surprised and very flattered, to say the least.

I highly recommend writing out your obituary with your family and friends before you go so you can edit and run it by everyone ahead of time because it's freaking stressful when people die. Having seen some examples, obituary writing isn't anyone's forte. It's not morbid. It's a public service.

I was typing on Grandma's desktop while Mom and Aunt Cathy looked on in encouragement. It could only be so long for the newspaper and we were constrained to 350 words. When her obituary appeared, I was horrified that I'd been censored so here is how it was meant to appear in its blasphemous entirety:

EMMA JEAN NORMAN
August 07, 1934 - February 19, 2016

Jean Norman went peacefully to her immortal home on February 19, 2016, and will not be making any more of "that damned applesauce."

Emma Jean Norman was born in Cadillac to Lillian (Samuelson) and Albert Smith on August 7, 1934. An accomplished baker, generous with peanut butter sheet cakes, molasses cookies, and blitz tortes, the fights over her spritz cookies at Christmastime will live on in our memories as will our love for her.

She graduated from Tustin High and married Darwin Norman on March 7, 1953. Jean had five children and helped Darwin run Darelnor Eggs before it closed in 1984. She worked at Network Reporting, Godfrey's of Cadillac, and Gary Trimarco's of Big Rapids. Jean was an active 4-H leader who helped many kids earn state awards in sewing. She also helped with Pine River Area Historical Society's calendar.

Jean loved musicals like *Oklahoma!* and *The Sound of Music*, wore "I love my grandkids" sweatshirts, and always had a craft project in the works along with a few loaves of bread rising in the kitchen.

She is survived by her husband of 63 years, Darwin; daughters: Margaret (Richard) Ecker of McMinnville, Oregon, Mary Ellen (Randy) Holmes of Tustin, Myra Norman of Cedar Springs; son, Mark (Catherine) Norman of Tustin; grandchildren Aaron (Kara) Ecker of Dayton, Oregon, Angela (Duane) Christie of Tustin, Zachary Holmes of Tustin, Summer (Lewis) Deline of Reed City, and Seth Norman of Tustin; great-grandchildren: Talon, Olivia, Torrigan, Neil, Henry, Jacob, Delaney and Brody, and the couples' two rescue dogs, Duke and Toby.

Jean was met in Heaven by her parents; siblings, Alberta (Robert) Bottje, Shirley (Nelbert) Pauley, Norman (Shirley) Smith, and Alvera (Elwood) Dahley, daughter Benita Norman, and grandson Daniel Ecker.

A Celebration of Life memorial will take place this summer for friends and family. In lieu of flowers, memorial contributions may be made to Munson Hospice of Cadillac or The Salvation Army.

"I want some French toast. We have enough French or do we have to make homemade?"

Damn Applesauce

It was never meant to be a defining moment in family history, but like all good things, it was here to stay. Grandma had been let go from her job. Someone younger was wanted and she was expected to train them before she was phased out. I'm not familiar with many labor laws but age discrimination still is a hard battle to win.

Since she was between jobs, she spent the whole summer at home with Grandpa. All-day. Every day. This new normal was hard to get accustomed to. She was used to going out every morning, keeping busy, and coming home late after grocery shopping

Somehow, though an unknown series of events, they started canning applesauce. I think Grandpa just wanted to keep her busy. It seemed like every time we stopped by their house; they were running apples through the Squeezo.

It was late in the summer when the entire family gathered for one of our many traditional birthday dinners. Since she was the guest of honor, someone asked Grandma what her plans were for the fall. She didn't have a clear course in mind but one thing was for sure she told us. "I'm not making any more of that damned apple sauce!"

She later got a new job at a car dealership and was alleviated of boredom and endless apple sauce production, but every get-together, every Thanksgiving, Christmas, and Easter there would be a jar of applesauce on the table available for consumption and we'd ask if it was damn applesauce. Regular store-bought applesauce simply isn't as full of resentment.

The Cereal Bowl

I debated on adding this as it's not usually what I write and I didn't want to alienate any atheist friends, but every now and then I feel moved to write a sermon. I sit down until the feeling passes as it's unneeded, I'm not qualified, nor do people really want to hear it. So, skip this part if you want.

We bought a plain white set of dishes after our house fire. They're nondescript and unremarkable. However, one has a chip in it. My children fight and argue over who has the chipped bowl. Yes, we've got bowls that aren't damaged and they work well and serve their purpose, but this bowl that has seen some damage and has been around the block is still good. He still holds cereal. He's been dropped on the tile floor and survived. His scars are what set him apart from the rest of the dishes. His flaws are what everyone clamors for.

God doesn't need you whole and perfect. All He asks for is you; chipped and dropped. Even if you're not a believer, this is for you. Anyone who feels their cracks and chips are holding them back, or if you feel flawed beyond repair and there's really nothing you're good for; if you don't even hold cereal you're so broken know this: your family, your friends, your co-workers, and acquaintances love and admire you.

Your perseverance and tenacity have brought you this far and your struggle and pain are beautiful. Your story is important. It shows others that they are not alone and if that cracked bowl is clamored over, you are wanted too despite everything.

The Bears I Dream Of

I was reading Erma Bombeck recently and she says it's not big things that ruin marriages, it's little things. Yes, Erma, yes! Girl, tell them how it is! The mayo/ salad dressing debates that occur whenever we make chicken, tuna, or awesome salad have almost led to the neighbors calling the authorities. For some reason condiments are where stands are made and lines are drawn in our house. Things get heated and tensions rise when someone hauls out the jar with the light blue lid instead of the Hellmann's.

In seventh grade, we read *Hatchet*. To supplement the lesson, the DNR came and spoke to us. We were also handed a newspaper article about the little girl in the Upper Peninsula who was hauled off the porch by a black bear, killed, and eaten. I was traumatized. After that article, I did what any normal autistic would do and learned everything about bear attacks. My mom would order me books from the back of Dad's hunting magazines. I'm still terrified of bears, but I have knowledge on my side now along with the sheer terror.

I average about two or three bear nightmares a year; however, on one particular night, cold dread filled me. I could hear a bear roaring and snarling even after I woke up. My heart started racing before I realized it was my husband's snoring. My husband sounds so much like a 400-pound beast of the wild he actually gives me nightmares. Most of the time I just muffle the sound with a hefty memory foam pillow placed lovingly and gently over his airways.

I offer no solution to overcoming little things in marriage even if they sound like big things that live in the woods. So, in closing, I leave you with a poem Neil wrote for me and also an awesome salad recipe.

> The bears I dream of
> The snoring I hear of
> All because of one

Cauliflower Broccoli Salad Recipe

Prep Time: 15 minutes Cook Time: 5 minutes
Total Time: 20 minutes
Servings: 6 servings

INGREDIENTS

3 cups raw cauliflower, small florets
3 cups raw broccoli, small florets
1/2 medium red onion, finely chopped
1 cup mild cheddar, grated
1/2 pack bacon, chopped & cooked (8 oz)
1/4 cup sunflower seeds
1/3 cup craisins (dried cranberries)
Dressing-

1 cup **mayonnaise**

1/3 cup granulated sugar
1/4 cup white vinegar

INSTRUCTIONS

Cook bacon pieces, set onto a paper towel to cool.
Cut broccoli and cauliflower into small florets. Finely chop the onion.
Prepare the homemade salad dressing. Combine the mayo, sugar, and vinegar.
In a bowl add the broccoli, cauliflower, cheese, sunflower seeds, cranberries, bacon, and red onion. Add dressing.
Combine well and enjoy!

"Mom, you know when Noah was on his ship?"

"Uh, yeah?"

"He was watching Star Wars and he was thirsty."

"He was thirsty?"

"Yeah. He wanted some orange juice."

Cleaner, Clearer Windows

In my heart, I feel dirty windows, full of smudges and mud-encrusted handprints, are actually a good thing. They have saved countless birds' lives at our house. Since giving up on the domestic arts, our wildlife has flourished. However, I do like a nice sunbeam on my couch to read in. I also don't want my plants to believe I'm terraforming on Mars and give up on me.

The first step to glorious glass is to call the orphanage. Seriously though you need a lint-free cloth. Paper towel is right out. I like microfiber myself. It's washable and reusable. Some swear by a newspaper.

Secondly, we don't use chemical sprays anymore. I like the nice vinegar/water mixture. If your kids aren't complaining about the vinegar smell, add more. Ideally, you should be able to clear a living room of tablet playing, Disney+ watching, zombies in seconds.

Thirdly, spray glass, and wipe in one direction. For example, wipe side to side and on the opposite side of the glass, swipe up and down that way if there are streaks, it's easy to see which side they occurred. If you're like me, you're now the proud owner of windows with a gingham streak pattern.

Lastly, enjoy the view for about two hours because a kid fresh from the sprinkler and covered in sunscreen will rub his entire body on the sliding glass door instead of knocking. If the boy fails at this, keep an eye out for the toddler and her jam covered hands.

Should your children let you down; the dog will cover your clean window in nose-prints while keeping you safe from the Murder Squirrels. Try not to make the neighbors jealous.

Defense Against the Domestic Arts

Who decided to call it the domestic arts? There's nothing artistic in scrubbing a toilet or emptying the kitchen drain of the wet mushy food that doesn't even resemble food anymore. You do it because you have to not because it fills you with joy and a sense of accomplishment. If it does, are you for hire?

Homemaking is a creative act, we're told; a work of art in progress. Cooking, cleaning, sewing, money management, raising children, first aid and basic health care, home décor, and home maintenance are domestic arts.

No. Staying alive isn't artistic. There's nothing noble about keeping your own living space clean especially when people are paid to do it outside of the home. I'd read an op-ed piece about how feminism in the twentieth century led to the rise of consumerism because women weren't staying home to cook and sew clothes.

Now I love to sew when the spirit moves me, but the thought of being responsible for clothing my entire family even post sewing machine gives me second-hand anxiety. 100 years ago, we'd be the poor family the community church worried about. I love making jam too, but because I want to do it not because we'd starve this winter if I didn't can and preserve everything we grew.

Childbearing is considered domestic art. Actually, making the babies was the easiest most enjoyable part, albeit messy. I fail to see how wiping butts and talking my toddler out of coloring her face with green marker is either righteous or congruent to us furthering the species.

I think part of me wishes I was better at housekeeping, but for now, for my sanity, that family of spiders by the ceiling vent get to stay a little longer. I don't know where that smell is coming from either so breath through your mouth next time you visit.

The Saints' Patience

I didn't move my daughter's little pink bathroom stool to where she wanted it when she wanted it. My cruelty borders on that of most stepmothers and all nefarious dictators both past and present.

My son's hot bath with foamy lavender honey bubble bath wasn't warm enough. "Can I drain it and start all over?" He whines. Maybe if he had to pump and haul the water and heat it himself, I wouldn't be banging my head against the wall in pure frustration.

These poor children and their first world problems. They all got new shoes this spring. You know what they wear? Nothing. No socks. No shoes. As long as it's climatically possible. Rain or shine.

I didn't realize when I signed up for strong-willed and independent children who'd change the world, I'd be getting it in spades. Seriously, all three could try the patience of a saint, the pope, a convent of nuns, and the late great Mr. J.C. himself. The Dalai Lama would remain neutral since needing patience seems to have more of a Catholic theme at this juncture.

Every day is a fight for passable hygiene and basic oral health. It's not socially acceptable to walk around looking and smelling like one's been dipped in jam and peanut butter respectively, then rolled down a hill of sand. It's just not cool to make people gag when you walk by.

I'd give up the fight, but they are my legacy and I don't want to be remembered as the mom whose kids smell like Fritos and look like they fell off a hay wagon, but if you should ever encounter children like those mentioned above please send them back home.

The Cats in My Dryer

Through no fault of mine, I have more to add to the Animal House vignette since it was written. Unbeknownst to me, our new house is also a B&B to all animals both wild and domestic. It was never my intention. I know some people who'd rather stuff their home with animals than children. We chose both, but I guess word got out that anything is welcome here.

I can't speak for other people, but I prefer to be surprised with breakfast in bed when I wake up. That day I was deeply ensconced in French toast when my husband came to me at the kitchen table with a little gray kitten in his arms. I found her in the dryer he tells me as fact. No friends, that is the last thing I expected to see let alone hear as syrup dribbled down my chins.

I've had my own share of half laundered cat encounters, but it was only because the dryer was still hot and full of clothes that were only slightly damp. Once I heard the first two clunks, I stopped all appliances and took a week off chores. Our cats have never been warm laundry devotees and after that Holli cat didn't do it again.

We leave the kitchen window slightly open because our polydactyl, Lily, and Neil's birthday kitty, Whiskers, are fierce hunters and devout lovers of mousy brains. They like to come and go all night. For now, it works for us and is the only conceivable way for the little girl kitten to have gotten in. Unless there is a vortex in the dryer that not only steals socks but also produces kittens.

The kids are ecstatic and are convinced we're keeping her. It will only be a matter of time before I find raccoons in the dining room buffet and porcupines under my bed.

Paparazzi

Lady Gaga once sang, "I'm your biggest fan, I'll follow you until you love me." And while I'll never achieve the fame or fortune Miss Gaga can acclaim, I know too how it feels to be relentlessly hounded, always pressed for my undivided attention. My name echoes through the house, the public needing me. There's just no click or flash from the cameras or paycheck from my intellectual brilliance.

I go to the grocery store and I hear the frantic calls from my fans in the toy aisle. Sure, when they pronounce Angela it sounds a lot like Mom, but popularity knows no boundaries and multisyllabic names are difficult when you're only three.

As I drive, they're at their worst coming at me from all angles especially since the oldest is big enough for the front seat now. "Look over here!" They shout, but as I am driving and we've never had chauffeur, they're just ignored unsuccessfully as I toss granola bars at them.

The questions shouted at me daily, as they wheedle secrets to sell to a gossipy tabloid, rival those at any press conference and they're never happy with a gruff, "No comment!"

"What's in a cat's eye?" It's a nictitating membrane. He's okay.

"What's the cutest thing ever?" Me! Next question.

"Is Dad going to work?" Dad always goes to work this hasn't changed in the last 24 hours.

"Where is Whiskers?" Off doing cat things. Lucky duck.

"Where's my phone?"

"Can I watch YouTube?"

"Who didn't flush? Gross boys!"

"Can I have a snack?"

"Can we do a project?"

Sometimes they try to address me with statements while disguising it as a question. "I have a question!" A child will state. "Yes?" I'll tentatively reply.

"Dominoes are just melted dice!"

I've attempted to establish healthy boundaries. I tried childproofing the house once, but they kept getting in.

"Mom, you know what a good baby name is?

Shostakovich!"

Unequally Yoked

My best friend grew up Baptist and when I'd go to her house for sleepovers, we would go to church Sunday mornings. Somehow the topic came up. It might have been because I was dating a Catholic, but she mentioned the verse in 2nd Corinthians about being unequally yoked with unbelievers.

Now a lot of people use this verse in defense of being the same religion in marriage. I'm here to tell you it has nothing to do with belief in the Almighty and everything to do with gaming; not the casino kind either.

You see, I grew up on Nintendo. My dad and grandma played Pac-Man on the Odyssey 2. Mom would play Dr. Mario with us. We had a Sega Genesis and when my brother reached his teen years, he bought a Sony PlayStation and a Nintendo 64. My grandma was known to drop it down on her Game

Boy with a fresh game of Tetris. Console games are in our blood.

My husband grew up playing computer games. He's a PC gamer, but there's nothing correct about always wearing out the aswd keys on the computer keyboard. He grew up with *Lemmings*, *Duke Nukem*, and *Diablo*. He plays *Skyrim* and *Guild Wars 2* on the regular.

Our boys like to watch people on YouTube play video games. Their favorite games are Minecraft and Terraria. I was highly flattered Uncle Zach hooked up the Raspberry Pi and they needed my help getting past Chemical Zone in *Sonic 2*. "Wow, Mom! It's like you play like a real gamer!" Neil tells us. Gee, thanks, son.

We currently don't own any console gaming devices. My husband refuses to even try them. It's been the biggest hurdle in our marriage besides the mayo thing. When one decides to yolk oneself to another make sure he/she/they are a die-hard console gamer.

The only yoke of equality we've had any luck with is in *Oregon Trail* from a floppy disk on an Apple from 1994. It is a classic. There's nothing like a yoke of oxen to ford the Kansas River. That we can agree on.

"Mom, we're all out of taco buns!"

(A child realizing we have no tortillas)

Night Maneuvers

Mad props to Mr. Seger and his band of ammunition. His works are no doubt legendary albeit now just as silver as said ammunition.

One tune, in particular, I never felt any affinity for was one about sweaty, angst-filled teenage sexy-times. To me, when I hear that particular title track, I'm hearkened back to the days before our house fire.

Ooh, I remember. Yeah, I remember. Autumn was closing in and squirrels had infiltrated our attic. Evenings were when they were most active and I could hear them scurrying across the attic floor all night long. I question why a battalion of squirrels chose our attic as headquarters and used it for training exercises, but what I do know was that the cat consistently awoke me at 3 a.m. each night to let her upstairs since everyone knows it's the tactically appropriate time to begin Black Ops on the squirrels.

Clearly, that's what motion in the night really means: strategic operations critical to the mission performed under the cover of darkness. The best part of an attic full of squirrels was it kept the kids out of old toys that had been packed away. One steadfast rule, possibly the only rule in our house, is something needs to be picked up if another toy set is to be gotten out. The boys would sneak upstairs and haul stuff down at random and with reckless abandon until the squirrels startled them so badly that Henry bounced down the stairs with all the grace of a stuntman as they screamed for me.

Sweet, sweet summertime! Those squirrels worked better than any locked door could. Their night moves kept my attic well-protected and complete negligence of the trusty woods was a bonus for me.

"What do you want for breakfast, Henry?"
(Sometimes we're a democratic household & the voter decides)

"A rainbow!"
(Sometimes voters are very uninformed and underage and we have a recount)

"Mom, I will make sure that Dad doesn't get any broccoli, so you can be more fartful."

About

A connoisseur of savory puns, Angela takes herself too seriously and is riddled with crippling self-doubt. She sees the humor in everything else, however, and laughs at more than what's respectable for someone with an unattractive smile and double chin.

Her lasting passions all contain too much sugar and carbohydrates for the general public. Angela feels nothing, NOTHING could have prepared her for the strenuous rigors of motherhood, and lays the blame at the feet of public education. Knowing and using the Pythagorean theorem is all well and good until you're being barfed on at 2a.m.

She has been married somewhat successfully since 2006 and has 3 children of various ages, temperaments, and abilities. They currently keep them themselves surrounded by a dog, three cats, and 12 chickens.

When she's not making homemade soap no one wants, Angela can be found scrolling Pinterest on the couch most afternoons and obsessing over jam recipes while she pretends her life is very successful.

www.ingramcontent.com/pod-product-compliance
Lightning Source LLC
Chambersburg PA
CBHW061445040426
42450CB00007B/1225